BBQ Chicken Pizza Cookbook
Delicious Recipes and Techniques for Crafting Irresistible BBQ Chicken Pizzas

While every precaution has been taken in the preparation of this book, the publisher assumes no responsibility for errors or omissions, or for damages resulting from the use of the information contained herein.

BBQ CHICKEN PIZZA COOKBOOK

First edition. November 1, 2023.

Copyright © 2023 john ahmad.

ISBN: 979-8223494706

Written by john ahmad.

John Ahmad

Outline:

The World of BBQ Chicken Pizza

- A Brief History of BBQ Chicken Pizza
- The Evolution of Flavors and Styles

Essential Ingredients and Tools

- Choosing the Right Chicken Cuts
- Selecting the Perfect BBQ Sauce
- Pizza Dough Variations and Tips
- Must-Have Pizza Making Tools

Homemade BBQ Sauce Recipes

- Classic Smoky BBQ Sauce
- Tangy and Spicy Kansas City BBQ Sauce
- Sweet and Zesty Pineapple BBQ Sauce

Pizza Dough Masterclass

- Basic Pizza Dough Recipe
- Whole Wheat Pizza Dough
- Gluten-Free Pizza Crust

Classic BBQ Chicken Pizza

- The All-Time Favorite Combination
- Perfecting the Cheese-to-Chicken Ratio

BBQ Chicken Pizza Variations

- BBQ Chicken and Bacon Pizza

Gluten-Free and Keto-Friendly Options

- Cauliflower Crust BBQ Chicken Pizza
- Low Carb BBQ Chicken Pizza

Breakfast Twist: BBQ Chicken Pizza for Brunch

- BBQ Chicken and Egg Breakfast Pizza
- Maple Syrup Drizzle for Sweetness

BBQ Dessert Pizza

- Decadent Nutella and BBQ Chicken Dessert Pizza
- Fruity Delight: BBQ Chicken and Berry Dessert Pizza

Aromatic Herbs and Seasonings

- Elevating Flavors with Fresh Herbs
- Unique Seasoning Blends for BBQ Chicken Pizza

Storing and Reheating Tips

- Keeping Leftover Pizza Fresh
- Creative Ways to Reheat BBQ Chicken Pizza

Hosting a BBQ Chicken Pizza Party

- Building a DIY Pizza Station
- Pairing Beverages with BBQ Chicken Pizza

Beyond Chicken: BBQ-Style Veggie Pizzas

- BBQ Cauliflower Pizza
- BBQ Portobello Mushroom Pizza

Final Thoughts and Culinary Adventures

- Tips for Customizing Your Own BBQ Chicken Pizzas
- Exploring Global BBQ Pizza Inspirations

Chapter 1: The World of BBQ Chicken Pizza

A Brief History of BBQ Chicken Pizza

Pizza has been a beloved dish for centuries, with its origins dating back to ancient civilizations. However, BBQ chicken pizza, a mouthwatering fusion of classic Italian pizza and tangy barbecue flavors, has a more recent and fascinating history.

1.1 The Emergence of BBQ Chicken Pizza

In the 1980s, on the sunny shores of California, a culinary revolution was quietly taking place. Pizzerias began experimenting with unconventional toppings, pushing the boundaries of traditional pizza recipes. It was during this period that the innovative idea of combining barbecue flavors with pizza was born.

One of the first establishments to pioneer BBQ chicken pizza was the legendary California Pizza Kitchen (CPK). Their chefs were inspired by the tangy and smoky flavors of barbecue sauce, and they decided to incorporate it into their pizza offerings. The result was a tantalizing combination that soon became a customer favorite.

1.2 The Innovators

The rise of BBQ chicken pizza wouldn't have been possible without the creative minds and daring palates of visionary chefs. Names like Ed LaDou, a renowned pizza chef, and co-founder of CPK, played a crucial role in popularizing this unique pizza variant. LaDou's willingness to experiment with various toppings, including grilled chicken and BBQ sauce, paved the way for the creation of a new pizza sensation.

1.3 Early Variations

As the concept of BBQ chicken pizza gained traction, different regions and pizzerias put their own spin on the dish. Some incorporated tangy and spicy barbecue sauce, while others experimented with sweet and smoky variations. Toppings like red onions, cilantro, and even pineapple were added to enhance the flavor profile, creating a diverse range of early BBQ chicken pizza recipes.

1.4 The Popularity Surge

By the 1990s, BBQ chicken pizza had become a mainstream hit across the United States. Its unique combination of flavors resonated with people from all walks of life, making it a staple on many pizza menus. Its popularity extended beyond the shores of California and reached pizza enthusiasts worldwide.

The evolution of BBQ chicken pizza did not stop there. As the years passed, various regional styles emerged, each with its distinct twist on the classic recipe. From Texas-style BBQ chicken pizza with a smoky kick to Carolina-style with a tangy vinegar-based sauce, the possibilities seemed endless.

Today, BBQ chicken pizza continues to be a favorite among pizza aficionados, and its legacy of culinary innovation remains strong. As more and more home cooks and pizzerias experiment with new ingredients and techniques, the flavors and styles of BBQ chicken pizza will continue to evolve, delighting taste buds and satisfying pizza cravings around the globe. So, let's embark on a culinary adventure, exploring the delicious recipes and techniques that will help you craft irresistible BBQ chicken pizzas in the comfort of your own kitchen. Get ready to savor the perfect blend of smoky, savory, and tangy flavors as we delve into the world of BBQ chicken pizza!

Chapter 2: Essential Ingredients and Tools

Creating the perfect BBQ chicken pizza requires a combination of high-quality ingredients and the right tools to bring out the best flavors and textures. In this chapter, we will explore the essential components that form the foundation of your BBQ chicken pizza masterpiece.

2.1 Choosing the Right Chicken Cuts

When it comes to BBQ chicken pizza, selecting the right chicken cuts is crucial to ensure that your pizza is packed with juicy, flavorful bites of chicken. While boneless, skinless chicken breasts are a popular choice due to their lean and versatile nature, you can also opt for boneless, skinless chicken thighs for a more tender and succulent result. Pre-marinated chicken strips can be a convenient option if you're looking to save time without compromising on taste.

When choosing chicken for your BBQ pizza, look for fresh, high-quality cuts. If possible, support local farmers or visit your nearby butcher to get the best cuts available. If you prefer a smokier flavor, consider using grilled or smoked chicken to elevate the taste of your pizza.

To prepare the chicken, you can marinate it in your favorite BBQ sauce for a few hours before cooking, ensuring that the flavors infuse deeply into the meat. Grilling or pan-searing the chicken will create those delectable charred edges that make BBQ chicken pizza truly special.

2.2 Selecting the Perfect BBQ Sauce

The key to a delectable BBQ chicken pizza is finding the perfect BBQ sauce that complements the flavors of both the chicken and the pizza itself. In this section, we'll explore the world of BBQ sauces, from the classic smoky and tangy varieties to the sweet and spicy renditions.

Each region boasts its own unique BBQ sauce style, such as the rich and molasses-based Kansas City sauce or the tangy and vinegar-forward Carolina sauce. When choosing a BBQ sauce, consider your personal taste preferences. If you enjoy a balance of sweet and savory, opt for a classic smoky BBQ sauce. For those who prefer a bit of heat, look for a sauce with a spicy kick.

You can experiment with store-bought BBQ sauces to find your favorite, or you can have fun creating your own signature BBQ sauce. Mixing and matching ingredients like ketchup, brown sugar, vinegar, mustard, and spices will allow you to tailor the sauce to your liking. Remember, the sauce will be the base of your pizza, so choose one that you truly enjoy.

2.3 Pizza Dough Variations and Tips

The pizza dough is the canvas on which you build your BBQ chicken pizza masterpiece. In this section, we'll explore various pizza dough variations that cater to different dietary needs and tastes. For traditional pizza lovers, we'll share a classic pizza dough recipe that yields a chewy and airy crust, perfect for holding all the delicious toppings.

To make classic pizza dough, you'll need simple ingredients such as all-purpose flour, yeast, water, olive oil, salt, and a touch of sugar. The process involves mixing and kneading the dough, allowing it to rise, and then shaping it into a perfect pizza crust.

For health-conscious pizza enthusiasts, we'll delve into whole wheat pizza dough, offering a heartier and nuttier flavor profile. Whole wheat flour adds nutritional value and a subtle rustic taste to the pizza. Additionally, we'll provide a gluten-free pizza crust option that maintains the integrity of the pizza while accommodating gluten-sensitive individuals.

To ensure your pizza dough turns out perfect every time, follow these essential tips:

- Use fresh yeast or active dry yeast to ensure proper dough rise.
- Let the dough rest and rise in a warm, draft-free place to activate

the yeast.

- Knead the dough until it becomes smooth and elastic to achieve the desired texture.
- Preheat your oven and pizza stone (if using one) to ensure a crisp and evenly cooked crust.
- Roll out the dough evenly to achieve a consistent thickness across the pizza.

By mastering these foundational skills, you'll be well on your way to creating a BBQ chicken pizza with a mouthwatering crust that enhances the flavors of the toppings.

2.4 Must-Have Pizza Making Tools

Equipping yourself with the right pizza-making tools can make a significant difference in the pizza-making process. In this section, we'll highlight the essential tools you need to create a fantastic BBQ chicken pizza at home.

Pizza Peel: A pizza peel is a flat, shovel-like tool used to slide the pizza into and out of the oven. It ensures a smooth transfer without deforming the pizza.

Pizza Stone: A pizza stone helps achieve that perfect crispy crust by distributing heat evenly and absorbing excess moisture from the dough.

Pizza Cutter: A sharp pizza cutter allows you to slice the pizza cleanly and efficiently, creating neat and appetizing slices.

Rolling Pin: A rolling pin is essential for rolling out your pizza dough to the desired thickness.

Pizza Pan or Baking Sheet: If you don't have a pizza stone, a pizza pan or baking sheet will suffice for baking your pizza.

Oven Thermometer: An oven thermometer ensures that your oven is at the correct temperature for optimal pizza baking.

Pastry Brush: A pastry brush is handy for brushing the crust with olive oil or garlic butter for added flavor.

Tongs: Tongs are useful for handling hot chicken or toppings during the pizza assembly.

Having these essential tools on hand will streamline the pizza-making process, making it easier and more enjoyable to create your BBQ chicken pizza.

With the knowledge of essential ingredients and tools in your arsenal, you're now ready to embark on your BBQ chicken pizza-making journey. Whether you're a seasoned pizza chef or a beginner in the kitchen, mastering these foundational elements will set the stage for crafting the most irresistible BBQ chicken pizzas you've ever tasted. Get ready to create pizzas that will leave your family and friends craving more!

Chapter 3: Homemade BBQ Sauce Recipes

One of the joys of making your own BBQ chicken pizza is having complete control over the flavors, and that begins with the BBQ sauce. In this chapter, we'll explore three mouthwatering homemade BBQ sauce recipes, each offering a unique twist on the classic flavors.

3.1 Classic Smoky BBQ Sauce

There's nothing quite like the rich and smoky flavors of a classic BBQ sauce. This versatile sauce serves as the perfect base for your BBQ chicken pizza, providing a perfect balance of sweet, tangy, and smoky notes. Let's gather the ingredients and create this timeless BBQ sauce that will elevate your pizza to new heights.

Ingredients:

- 1 cup ketchup
- 1/4 cup apple cider vinegar
- 1/4 cup dark brown sugar
- 2 tablespoons molasses
- 2 tablespoons Worcestershire sauce
- 1 tablespoon Dijon mustard
- 1 teaspoon smoked paprika
- 1/2 teaspoon garlic powder
- 1/2 teaspoon onion powder
- 1/4 teaspoon cayenne pepper (optional, for a spicy kick)
- Salt and pepper to taste

Instructions:

1. In a saucepan over medium heat, combine all the ingredients, stirring well to ensure they are thoroughly mixed.
2. Bring the mixture to a simmer, then reduce the heat to low and

let it simmer for 10-15 minutes, stirring occasionally to prevent burning.

3. Taste the sauce and adjust the seasoning according to your preference, adding more salt, pepper, or cayenne pepper for additional heat.

4. Remove the sauce from the heat and let it cool before using it on your BBQ chicken pizza.

This classic smoky BBQ sauce will infuse your pizza with the familiar, comforting flavors of traditional barbecue while complementing the tangy chicken and cheese.

3.2 Tangy and Spicy Kansas City BBQ Sauce

Known for its bold and robust flavors, the Kansas City BBQ sauce is a favorite among barbecue enthusiasts. This tangy and slightly spicy sauce is a delightful addition to BBQ chicken pizza, adding a zesty kick that balances perfectly with the sweetness of the sauce. Let's dive into the recipe and create this sensational Kansas City-style sauce.

Ingredients:

- 1 cup ketchup
- 1/2 cup apple cider vinegar
- 1/4 cup dark brown sugar
- 2 tablespoons molasses
- 2 tablespoons honey
- 1 tablespoon soy sauce
- 1 tablespoon chili powder
- 1 teaspoon smoked paprika
- 1/2 teaspoon garlic powder
- 1/2 teaspoon onion powder
- 1/4 teaspoon cayenne pepper (adjust for desired spiciness)
- Salt and pepper to taste

Instructions:

1. In a saucepan over medium heat, combine all the ingredients, stirring until well combined.
2. Bring the mixture to a gentle simmer, then reduce the heat to low and let it simmer for 10-15 minutes, allowing the flavors to meld together.
3. Taste the sauce and adjust the seasoning to your liking, adding more salt, pepper, or cayenne pepper for additional heat.
4. Once the sauce reaches the desired consistency, remove it from the heat and let it cool before using it as a delectable base for your BBQ chicken pizza.

With its tantalizing combination of tanginess and spiciness, this Kansas City BBQ sauce will elevate your pizza experience to a whole new level of flavor excitement.

3.3 Sweet and Zesty Pineapple BBQ Sauce

If you're a fan of tropical flavors, the sweet and zesty pineapple BBQ sauce is an absolute must-try for your BBQ chicken pizza. Bursting with fruity goodness and a hint of zing, this sauce adds a refreshing twist to the traditional BBQ chicken pizza. Let's gather the ingredients and create this delightful pineapple-infused BBQ sauce.

Ingredients:

- 1 cup ketchup
- 1/2 cup pineapple juice
- 1/4 cup dark brown sugar
- 2 tablespoons soy sauce
- 2 tablespoons apple cider vinegar
- 1 tablespoon molasses
- 1 teaspoon ground ginger
- 1/2 teaspoon garlic powder
- 1/2 teaspoon onion powder
- 1/4 teaspoon cayenne pepper (optional, for a spicy kick)
- Salt and pepper to taste

Instructions:

1. In a saucepan over medium heat, combine all the ingredients, stirring until well blended.
2. Bring the mixture to a gentle simmer, then reduce the heat to low and let it simmer for 10-15 minutes to allow the flavors to meld together.
3. Taste the sauce and adjust the seasoning according to your preference, adding more salt, pepper, or cayenne pepper for extra heat.
4. Remove the sauce from the heat and let it cool before using it on your BBQ chicken pizza.

The sweet and zesty pineapple BBQ sauce brings a burst of tropical goodness to your pizza, making it a memorable and delicious experience for your taste buds.

Now that you have these delectable homemade BBQ sauce recipes, your BBQ chicken pizza will be elevated to new culinary heights. These sauces offer a diverse range of flavors, ensuring that each pizza you make will be a unique and satisfying creation. So, get ready to indulge in the enticing world of homemade BBQ sauces and savor the mouthwatering results they bring to your BBQ chicken pizza!

Chapter 4: Pizza Dough Masterclass

The foundation of any great pizza is the dough, and mastering the art of pizza dough is essential for creating the perfect BBQ chicken pizza. In this chapter, we'll explore a pizza dough masterclass, providing you with three versatile recipes that cater to different dietary needs and tastes.

4.1 Basic Pizza Dough Recipe

A classic pizza dough is a blank canvas that allows the flavors of your BBQ chicken and sauce to shine. This basic pizza dough recipe will give you a soft and chewy crust, perfect for holding all your favorite toppings.

Ingredients:

- 2 1/4 cups all-purpose flour
- 1 teaspoon active dry yeast
- 1 cup warm water
- 2 tablespoons olive oil
- 1 teaspoon sugar
- 1 teaspoon salt

Instructions:

1. In a small bowl, combine warm water, sugar, and active dry yeast. Let it sit for 5-10 minutes until the yeast becomes frothy.
2. In a large mixing bowl, combine flour and salt. Gradually pour in the yeast mixture and olive oil.
3. Stir the ingredients together until a dough begins to form.
4. Transfer the dough onto a floured surface and knead for about 5-7 minutes until the dough is smooth and elastic.
5. Place the dough in a lightly oiled bowl, cover it with a damp cloth, and let it rise in a warm, draft-free area for about 1-2 hours or until it doubles in size.
6. After the dough has risen, punch it down to remove excess air.

Divide it into two equal portions to make two 12-inch pizzas.

7. Roll out each portion of dough into a 12-inch circle on a floured surface, then transfer it to a pizza peel or baking sheet, ready to add your BBQ chicken pizza toppings.

4.2 Whole Wheat Pizza Dough

For those who prefer a heartier and nuttier crust, whole wheat pizza dough is an excellent choice. Whole wheat flour adds a nutritious twist to your BBQ chicken pizza, creating a wholesome and flavorful base.

Ingredients:

- 1 1/2 cups whole wheat flour
- 1 cup all-purpose flour
- 1 packet (2 1/4 teaspoons) active dry yeast
- 1 cup warm water
- 2 tablespoons olive oil
- 1 teaspoon sugar
- 1 teaspoon salt

Instructions:

1. In a small bowl, combine warm water, sugar, and active dry yeast. Let it sit for 5-10 minutes until the yeast becomes frothy.
2. In a large mixing bowl, combine whole wheat flour, all-purpose flour, and salt. Gradually pour in the yeast mixture and olive oil.
3. Stir the ingredients together until a dough begins to form.
4. Transfer the dough onto a floured surface and knead for about 5-7 minutes until the dough is smooth and elastic.
5. Place the dough in a lightly oiled bowl, cover it with a damp cloth, and let it rise in a warm, draft-free area for about 1-2 hours or until it doubles in size.
6. After the dough has risen, punch it down to remove excess air.

Divide it into two equal portions to make two 12-inch pizzas.

7. Roll out each portion of dough into a 12-inch circle on a floured surface, then transfer it to a pizza peel or baking sheet, ready to add your BBQ chicken pizza toppings.

4.3 Gluten-Free Pizza Crust

For those with gluten sensitivity or those seeking a lighter alternative, a gluten-free pizza crust is the perfect solution. This recipe ensures that you can still enjoy a delectable BBQ chicken pizza without compromising on taste or texture.

Ingredients:

- 1 1/2 cups gluten-free all-purpose flour blend
- 1 teaspoon xanthan gum (if not already included in the flour blend)
- 1 packet (2 1/4 teaspoons) active dry yeast
- 1 cup warm water
- 2 tablespoons olive oil
- 1 teaspoon sugar
- 1 teaspoon salt

Instructions:

1. In a small bowl, combine warm water, sugar, and active dry yeast. Let it sit for 5-10 minutes until the yeast becomes frothy.
2. In a large mixing bowl, combine gluten-free all-purpose flour blend, xanthan gum (if needed), and salt. Gradually pour in the yeast mixture and olive oil.
3. Stir the ingredients together until a dough begins to form.
4. Transfer the dough onto a floured surface and knead for about 5-7 minutes until the dough is smooth and elastic.
5. Place the dough in a lightly oiled bowl, cover it with a damp cloth, and let it rise in a warm, draft-free area for about 1-2

hours or until it doubles in size.

6. After the dough has risen, punch it down to remove excess air. Divide it into two equal portions to make two 12-inch pizzas.

7. Roll out each portion of dough into a 12-inch circle on a floured surface, then transfer it to a pizza peel or baking sheet, ready to add your BBQ chicken pizza toppings.

By mastering these three pizza dough recipes, you'll have the flexibility to create BBQ chicken pizzas that cater to various dietary preferences. Whether you opt for the classic pizza dough, the heartiness of whole wheat, or the gluten-free option, you'll have a delicious and customized base for your BBQ chicken pizza masterpiece. So, let's roll up our sleeves and prepare the perfect pizza dough for an unforgettable BBQ chicken pizza experience!

Chapter 5: Classic BBQ Chicken Pizza

The Classic BBQ Chicken Pizza is an all-time favorite, loved by pizza enthusiasts for its irresistible blend of tangy BBQ sauce, tender chicken, and gooey cheese. In this chapter, we'll dive into the secrets of creating the perfect Classic BBQ Chicken Pizza and achieving the ideal cheese-to-chicken ratio for a mouthwatering pizza experience.

5.1 The All-Time Favorite Combination

The Classic BBQ Chicken Pizza brings together the flavors of barbecue and pizza in perfect harmony. The tangy and smoky BBQ sauce pairs beautifully with tender pieces of grilled chicken, while the melted cheese adds a luscious creaminess to each bite.

To create this pizza, start with your prepared pizza dough from the Pizza Dough Masterclass in Chapter 4. Spread a generous amount of your chosen BBQ sauce (such as the Classic Smoky BBQ Sauce from Chapter 3) onto the dough, leaving a small border around the edges. This base of rich and savory BBQ sauce will serve as the flavor foundation for your pizza.

Next, add a layer of shredded mozzarella cheese over the sauce. The mozzarella will melt beautifully during baking, providing a creamy and cheesy complement to the tangy BBQ sauce and chicken.

Now, it's time to add the star ingredient - the BBQ chicken. Remember the chicken cuts you chose from Chapter 2? Whether it's grilled chicken breast, smoky thighs, or marinated strips, place the cooked chicken pieces evenly across the pizza. Be generous with the chicken, ensuring that every slice will have a satisfying amount of meat.

To add a pop of color and freshness, consider adding thinly sliced red onions or fresh cilantro as optional toppings. These ingredients will provide a pleasant contrast to the richness of the BBQ sauce and cheese, adding a delightful twist to the classic combination.

Finally, transfer your pizza onto a preheated pizza stone in a hot oven or directly onto a preheated baking sheet. Bake until the crust is golden and the cheese is bubbly and slightly browned.

5.2 Perfecting the Cheese-to-Chicken Ratio

Achieving the perfect cheese-to-chicken ratio is a crucial element in creating a standout Classic BBQ Chicken Pizza. You want each bite to be balanced, ensuring that the cheese doesn't overpower the chicken or vice versa.

To strike this balance, start with a generous layer of shredded mozzarella cheese. The cheese acts as the binding agent between the crust and toppings, creating a cohesive and indulgent pizza experience.

As for the BBQ chicken, it's essential to distribute the chicken pieces evenly across the pizza. Aim to have a generous scattering of chicken, so every slice is loaded with meaty goodness.

Remember that the chicken will be the main protein source on this pizza, so don't shy away from adding a substantial amount. The combination of the tangy BBQ sauce, tender chicken, and melty cheese is what makes this pizza a classic favorite, and getting the cheese-to-chicken ratio just right will elevate the overall flavor and texture.

With your Classic BBQ Chicken Pizza fresh out of the oven, allow it to cool slightly before cutting into slices and serving. The harmony of flavors and the satisfying cheese-to-chicken ratio will make this pizza a surefire hit at any gathering or a delightful treat for a cozy night at home.

Now that you've mastered the art of creating a Classic BBQ Chicken Pizza and perfected the cheese-to-chicken ratio, you're ready to enjoy this timeless pizza classic. Savor each bite, and embrace the delightful blend of BBQ and pizza flavors that will leave you wanting more. So, let's raise a slice to the classic combination that continues to capture the hearts and taste buds of pizza lovers everywhere!

Chapter 6: BBQ Chicken Pizza Variations

While the Classic BBQ Chicken Pizza is undeniably delicious, there's a world of creative possibilities to explore with different toppings and flavor combinations. In this chapter, we'll introduce three mouthwatering BBQ Chicken Pizza variations that will excite your taste buds and take your pizza game to a whole new level.

6.1 BBQ Chicken and Bacon Pizza

The BBQ Chicken and Bacon Pizza is a delectable fusion of sweet and savory flavors. The smoky bacon adds a crispy texture and a burst of savory goodness, making it an irresistible combination with the tangy BBQ chicken.

To create this variation, start with the same BBQ chicken base as described in Chapter 5. You can use any of the homemade BBQ sauces, such as the Classic Smoky BBQ Sauce or the Tangy and Spicy Kansas City BBQ Sauce from Chapter 3.

After spreading the BBQ sauce on the pizza dough, add a generous layer of shredded mozzarella cheese. Then, top the pizza with your cooked BBQ chicken and evenly distribute crispy bacon pieces on top.

For a little extra kick, consider adding thinly sliced red onions or green onions for a hint of sharpness that complements the sweetness of the BBQ sauce. After baking the pizza to perfection, the marriage of tangy BBQ chicken, smoky bacon, and creamy cheese will be a true crowd-pleaser.

6.2 BBQ Chicken and Pineapple Pizza

Embrace a taste of the tropics with the BBQ Chicken and Pineapple Pizza variation. The sweetness of the pineapple balances the tangy BBQ sauce, creating a harmonious blend of flavors that transport you to a sunny paradise.

To create this tropical delight, once again, use your preferred BBQ chicken base from Chapter 5. The Classic Smoky BBQ Sauce or the Sweet and Zesty Pineapple BBQ Sauce from Chapter 3 would pair exceptionally well in this variation.

After spreading the sauce on the pizza dough, add a layer of shredded mozzarella cheese. Then, distribute the cooked BBQ chicken evenly across the pizza.

Now, the star of the show: add generous amounts of pineapple chunks to the pizza. The juicy and sweet pineapple perfectly complements the savory BBQ chicken, creating a taste sensation that's hard to resist.

For an added touch of brightness and flavor, consider adding sliced red bell peppers or jalapeños to provide a hint of spiciness. After baking, your BBQ Chicken and Pineapple Pizza will be a tropical delight that will whisk your taste buds away to a vacation in every bite.

6.3 BBQ Chicken and Jalapeño Pizza

If you're a fan of bold and spicy flavors, the BBQ Chicken and Jalapeño Pizza variation will satisfy your craving for heat. The spicy kick of jalapeños enhances the tanginess of the BBQ sauce, creating a pizza with a fiery punch.

To create this spicy masterpiece, use your favorite BBQ chicken base from Chapter 5. The Tangy and Spicy Kansas City BBQ Sauce or the Classic Smoky BBQ Sauce from Chapter 3 will be an excellent choice for this variation.

After spreading the BBQ sauce on the pizza dough, add a layer of shredded mozzarella cheese. Then, distribute the cooked BBQ chicken evenly on the pizza.

Now comes the fiery element: thinly slice fresh jalapeños and scatter them across the pizza. The amount of jalapeños you use can be adjusted to suit your spice tolerance, but the heat will certainly add an exciting dimension to your BBQ chicken pizza.

For a cooling contrast to the heat, consider adding dollops of creamy ranch dressing or crumbled blue cheese on top. After baking, your BBQ Chicken and Jalapeño Pizza will be a flavorful and spicy sensation that will keep you coming back for more.

With these tantalizing BBQ Chicken Pizza variations, you can embark on a flavor adventure with each new creation. Whether you prefer the smoky and savory combination of bacon, the tropical sweetness of pineapple, or the fiery kick of jalapeños, these variations showcase the endless possibilities of BBQ chicken pizza. So, get creative, and let your taste buds guide you as you explore the delightful world of BBQ Chicken Pizza Variations!

Chapter 7: Regional Twists on BBQ Chicken Pizza

Barbecue traditions vary across different regions of the United States, each boasting its unique flair and flavor profiles. In this chapter, we'll explore three regional twists on BBQ Chicken Pizza that draw inspiration from Texas, Memphis, and Carolina, each delivering a distinct and tantalizing taste experience.

7.1 Texas-Style BBQ Chicken Pizza

Texas is renowned for its bold and robust barbecue flavors, often centered around smoky, mesquite-cooked meats. The Texas-Style BBQ Chicken Pizza brings this rich barbecue heritage to your pizza, creating a savory and smoky delight.

To craft this Texas-inspired masterpiece, begin with your BBQ chicken base from Chapter 5. The Classic Smoky BBQ Sauce or the Tangy and Spicy Kansas City BBQ Sauce from Chapter 3 can serve as an excellent foundation.

After spreading the sauce on the pizza dough, add a layer of shredded smoked Gouda cheese. The smoky Gouda perfectly complements the grilled chicken and enhances the Texas-style experience.

Next, incorporate some traditional Texas barbecue elements. Consider adding sliced red onions, pickled jalapeños, and fresh cilantro to the pizza. These ingredients capture the essence of Texas barbecue, infusing your pizza with a medley of bold and savory flavors.

After baking to perfection, the Texas-Style BBQ Chicken Pizza will have your taste buds singing with delight, as you savor the distinctive smoky essence that makes Texas barbecue so beloved.

7.2 Memphis BBQ Chicken Pizza

Memphis barbecue is known for its tangy and sweet flavors, often accompanied by slow-cooked, tender meats. The Memphis BBQ Chicken Pizza pays homage to this style, delivering a harmonious balance of tanginess and sweetness.

To create this Memphis-inspired masterpiece, use your preferred BBQ chicken base from Chapter 5. The Sweet and Zesty Pineapple BBQ Sauce or the Classic Smoky BBQ Sauce from Chapter 3 will provide the ideal foundation for the Memphis twist.

After spreading the sauce on the pizza dough, add a layer of shredded cheddar cheese. The cheddar's sharpness complements the tangy sauce and adds depth to the overall flavor profile.

For a true Memphis experience, incorporate some classic Memphis barbecue toppings. Consider adding sliced red onions and green bell peppers to the pizza. These ingredients provide a pleasant crunch and enhance the sweetness of the barbecue sauce.

To achieve that perfect Memphis touch, sprinkle a light dusting of brown sugar over the pizza before baking. This little trick adds an extra layer of sweetness that is characteristic of Memphis barbecue.

After baking, the Memphis BBQ Chicken Pizza will be a symphony of sweet and tangy flavors, reminiscent of the cherished traditions of Memphis barbecue.

7.3 Carolina BBQ Chicken Pizza

Carolina barbecue is renowned for its vinegar-based sauces, offering a delightful tangy kick that sets it apart from other regional styles. The Carolina BBQ Chicken Pizza captures this tangy essence, infusing your pizza with a burst of acidity.

To create this Carolina-inspired masterpiece, once again, use your preferred BBQ chicken base from Chapter 5. The Tangy and Spicy Kansas City BBQ Sauce or the Sweet and Zesty Pineapple BBQ Sauce from Chapter 3 will pair harmoniously with the Carolina twist.

After spreading the sauce on the pizza dough, add a layer of shredded mozzarella cheese. The mozzarella's creamy texture provides a neutral base for the tangy flavors to shine.

For an authentic Carolina experience, incorporate some traditional Carolina barbecue toppings. Consider adding pickled red onions and a generous scattering of chopped pickles to the pizza. These ingredients amplify the tangy goodness and add a delightful zing to your pizza.

To enhance the Carolina twist, consider sprinkling a pinch of red pepper flakes over the pizza before baking. This touch of heat will complement the tangy flavors and elevate your Carolina BBQ Chicken Pizza to new heights.

After baking, the Carolina BBQ Chicken Pizza will leave you with a zesty and tangy flavor explosion that captures the essence of Carolina barbecue.

With these regional twists on BBQ Chicken Pizza, you can embark on a journey through the rich and diverse barbecue traditions of Texas, Memphis, and Carolina. Each variation celebrates the unique flavors that have made these regional styles beloved by barbecue enthusiasts worldwide. So, grab a slice and experience the distinct taste of each region with every bite of these regional BBQ Chicken Pizza variations!

Chapter 8: Grilled BBQ Chicken Pizzas

Grilling adds a smoky and charred flavor that takes BBQ chicken pizza to a whole new level. In this chapter, we'll explore the art of Grilled BBQ Chicken Pizzas, utilizing the grill to infuse your pizza with extra flavor and share tips for grilling pizza to perfection.

8.1 Utilizing the Grill for Extra Flavor

Grilling your BBQ chicken pizza adds a wonderful smoky depth to the flavors, creating a unique and irresistible taste experience. The high heat of the grill not only cooks the pizza crust to perfection but also caramelizes the BBQ sauce, intensifying its flavors.

To get started, preheat your grill to medium-high heat. You want the grill hot enough to cook the pizza quickly, but not too hot that it burns the crust or toppings.

Prepare your pizza dough and toppings as you would for a traditional oven-baked pizza. Once your dough is ready, roll it out into desired pizza sizes and thickness, making sure it's not too thin to avoid burning on the grill.

Before placing the pizza on the grill, lightly brush one side of the dough with olive oil to prevent sticking. Gently place the oiled side of the dough onto the preheated grill grates, oil-side down. Grill the dough for about 1-2 minutes or until it develops grill marks and begins to puff up.

Next, flip the dough using a pair of tongs or a large spatula. Now comes the fun part - adding your BBQ sauce, cheese, and BBQ chicken toppings directly onto the grilled side of the pizza.

Once the toppings are in place, close the grill lid to allow the cheese to melt and the toppings to cook. The pizza will be ready in just a few minutes, depending on your grill's heat and the thickness of the dough.

8.2 Tips for Grilling Pizza to Perfection

Grilling pizza can be a bit of an art, but with these tips, you'll be grilling BBQ chicken pizzas like a pro:

Preheat the grill: Make sure your grill is preheated to medium-high heat before placing the pizza dough on it. A well-heated grill will help achieve a nicely cooked crust and prevent sticking.

Keep toppings ready: Have all your toppings prepped and ready to go before placing the dough on the grill. Grilling pizza is a quick process, so you'll want everything at arm's reach to assemble the pizza swiftly.

Use indirect heat: For larger or thicker pizzas, consider using indirect heat by turning off one side of the grill or placing a pizza stone on the grill. This helps prevent the crust from burning while allowing the toppings to cook.

Don't overload the pizza: While it's tempting to add plenty of toppings, keep in mind that a heavily loaded pizza may take longer to cook, and the crust may not crisp up as well. Aim for a balanced amount of toppings to ensure even cooking.

Monitor the grill temperature: Keep an eye on the grill temperature to avoid burning the crust or toppings. Adjust the heat as needed to maintain a steady cooking temperature.

Remove from the grill carefully: Use a pizza peel or a large spatula to carefully remove the grilled pizza from the grill. Avoid using a fork, as it may puncture the crust and cause the toppings to slide off.

Grilling BBQ chicken pizzas is a delightful way to enjoy the smoky and charred flavors of outdoor cooking while savoring the delicious combination of BBQ chicken, tangy sauce, and melted cheese. With the right techniques and attention to detail, you'll master the art of grilling pizza to perfection, impressing your family and friends with each delightful slice. So, fire up the grill, and get ready to experience the magic of Grilled BBQ Chicken Pizzas!

Chapter 9: Creative BBQ Chicken Pizza Recipes

Embrace your culinary creativity with these innovative BBQ Chicken Pizza recipes. From a luscious BBQ Chicken Alfredo Pizza to a refreshing BBQ Chicken Caesar Salad Pizza, and a savory BBQ Chicken Calzone, these inventive recipes will surprise and delight your taste buds.

9.1 BBQ Chicken Alfredo Pizza

The BBQ Chicken Alfredo Pizza combines the best of two worlds: the indulgent creaminess of Alfredo sauce and the bold flavors of BBQ chicken. This fusion of flavors creates a pizza that's rich, flavorful, and utterly satisfying.

Ingredients:

- Prepared pizza dough (from Chapter 4)
- 1 cup cooked and shredded BBQ chicken
- 1 cup Alfredo sauce
- 1 1/2 cups shredded mozzarella cheese
- 1/2 cup sliced red onions
- Fresh parsley for garnish

Instructions:

1. Preheat your oven to the recommended temperature for pizza baking.
2. Roll out the pizza dough to your desired thickness and size.
3. Spread a layer of Alfredo sauce over the pizza dough, leaving a small border around the edges.
4. Sprinkle half of the shredded mozzarella cheese evenly over the Alfredo sauce.

5. Spread the cooked and shredded BBQ chicken across the pizza.
6. Add the sliced red onions on top of the BBQ chicken.
7. Finish with the remaining mozzarella cheese to help bind the toppings together.
8. Transfer the pizza onto a preheated pizza stone or a baking sheet.
9. Bake the pizza in the preheated oven until the crust is golden and the cheese is bubbly and slightly browned.
10. Garnish with fresh parsley before serving.

The BBQ Chicken Alfredo Pizza delivers a delightful fusion of creamy Alfredo sauce, tangy BBQ chicken, and melty cheese. This creative combination is sure to become a new favorite for pizza night.

9.2 BBQ Chicken Caesar Salad Pizza

The BBQ Chicken Caesar Salad Pizza brings the fresh and vibrant flavors of a Caesar salad to your pizza. It's a perfect balance of crispness and zestiness, making it a refreshing and satisfying meal.

Ingredients:

- Prepared pizza dough (from Chapter 4)
- 1 cup cooked and shredded BBQ chicken
- 1/2 cup Caesar salad dressing
- 1 1/2 cups shredded mozzarella cheese
- 1 cup chopped romaine lettuce
- 1/4 cup grated Parmesan cheese
- Croutons for garnish

Instructions:

1. Preheat your oven to the recommended temperature for pizza baking.
2. Roll out the pizza dough to your desired thickness and size.
3. Spread a layer of Caesar salad dressing over the pizza dough, leaving a small border around the edges.
4. Sprinkle half of the shredded mozzarella cheese evenly over the dressing.
5. Spread the cooked and shredded BBQ chicken across the pizza.
6. Add the remaining mozzarella cheese on top of the BBQ chicken.
7. Transfer the pizza onto a preheated pizza stone or a baking sheet.
8. Bake the pizza in the preheated oven until the crust is golden and the cheese is bubbly and slightly browned.
9. Remove the pizza from the oven and let it cool slightly.
10. Before serving, top the pizza with chopped romaine lettuce, grated Parmesan cheese, and a scattering of croutons for added

texture and freshness.

The BBQ Chicken Caesar Salad Pizza is a unique twist on traditional pizza, delivering the zesty flavors of Caesar salad combined with the tangy BBQ chicken. This creative recipe will impress both salad lovers and pizza enthusiasts alike.

9.3 BBQ Chicken Calzone

The BBQ Chicken Calzone is a delightful handheld treat that encases the goodness of BBQ chicken, cheese, and sauce in a golden-brown crust. It's a satisfying and portable alternative to traditional pizza.

Ingredients:

- Prepared pizza dough (from Chapter 4)
- 1 cup cooked and shredded BBQ chicken
- 1 cup marinara sauce or your favorite pizza sauce
- 1 1/2 cups shredded mozzarella cheese
- 1/2 cup sliced red onions
- Olive oil for brushing
- Garlic powder for sprinkling
- Dried oregano for sprinkling

Instructions:

1. Preheat your oven to the recommended temperature for pizza baking.
2. Divide the pizza dough into two equal portions.
3. Roll out each portion into a circle, about 10 inches in diameter.
4. On one half of each dough circle, layer the marinara or pizza sauce, leaving a small border around the edges.
5. Sprinkle half of the shredded mozzarella cheese over the sauce.
6. Add the cooked and shredded BBQ chicken on top of the cheese.

7. Add the sliced red onions on top of the BBQ chicken.
8. Fold the other half of the dough over the toppings to create a half-moon shape.
9. Use a fork to crimp the edges of the calzone to seal it shut.
10. Brush the top of each calzone with olive oil and sprinkle with garlic powder and dried oregano.
11. Transfer the calzones onto a baking sheet.
12. Bake in the preheated oven until the calzones are golden brown and crisp on the outside.
13. Remove from the oven and let them cool slightly before serving.

The BBQ Chicken Calzone is a fun and creative way to enjoy the flavors of BBQ chicken pizza in a convenient handheld form. The golden, flaky crust and melty cheese make this calzone a satisfying treat for any occasion.

With these creative BBQ Chicken Pizza recipes, you can add a touch of innovation to your pizza repertoire. Whether you opt for the luscious BBQ Chicken Alfredo Pizza, the refreshing BBQ Chicken Caesar Salad Pizza, or the savory BBQ Chicken Calzone, each recipe brings its unique twist to the beloved BBQ chicken pizza. So, let your culinary imagination run wild and enjoy the delectable journey of exploring these inventive BBQ Chicken Pizza recipes!

Chapter 10: Veggie Lovers' BBQ Chicken Pizza

Vegetarians and veggie enthusiasts alike can indulge in the delightful Veggie Lovers' BBQ Chicken Pizza. This chapter explores how to incorporate a variety of fresh and roasted vegetables to create a medley of colors and flavors that perfectly complement the tangy BBQ chicken.

10.1 Incorporating Fresh and Roasted Vegetables

The Veggie Lovers' BBQ Chicken Pizza celebrates the abundance of vegetables by combining both fresh and roasted varieties. The freshness of the vegetables adds a burst of color and texture, while roasting intensifies their flavors, making each bite a delightful experience.

Ingredients:

- Prepared pizza dough (from Chapter 4)
- 1 cup cooked and shredded BBQ chicken
- 1 cup BBQ sauce of your choice (from Chapter 3)
- 1 1/2 cups shredded mozzarella cheese
- 1/2 cup sliced red onions
- 1/2 cup sliced bell peppers (a mix of red, green, and yellow)
- 1/2 cup sliced mushrooms
- 1/4 cup roasted corn kernels
- Fresh basil leaves for garnish

Instructions:

1. Preheat your oven to the recommended temperature for pizza baking.
2. Roll out the pizza dough to your desired thickness and size.
3. Spread a layer of BBQ sauce over the pizza dough, leaving a small border around the edges.

4. Sprinkle half of the shredded mozzarella cheese evenly over the sauce.
5. Spread the cooked and shredded BBQ chicken across the pizza.
6. Add the sliced red onions, bell peppers, and mushrooms on top of the BBQ chicken.
7. Sprinkle the roasted corn kernels over the pizza.
8. Finish with the remaining mozzarella cheese, ensuring all the toppings are well-distributed.
9. Transfer the pizza onto a preheated pizza stone or a baking sheet.
10. Bake the pizza in the preheated oven until the crust is golden and the cheese is bubbly and slightly browned.
11. Remove the pizza from the oven and let it cool slightly.
12. Before serving, garnish the pizza with fresh basil leaves, adding a touch of freshness and brightness to the medley of flavors.

10.2 A Medley of Colors and Flavors

The Veggie Lovers' BBQ Chicken Pizza is a feast for the eyes and the palate, boasting a vibrant medley of colors and flavors that will captivate your senses.

The combination of red onions, bell peppers, mushrooms, and roasted corn kernels brings a variety of textures and tastes to the pizza. The sweetness of the roasted corn complements the savory BBQ chicken, while the bell peppers add a delightful crunch and a pop of color. The earthiness of the mushrooms and the sharpness of the red onions round out the medley of flavors, creating a harmonious balance on each slice.

The freshness of the vegetables adds a delightful contrast to the tangy BBQ sauce and the creamy mozzarella cheese, elevating the pizza into a Veggie Lovers' paradise.

Whether you're a dedicated vegetarian or simply looking to explore a veggie-packed pizza, the Veggie Lovers' BBQ Chicken Pizza is sure to satisfy your cravings for a flavorful and wholesome meal.

Chapter 11: BBQ Chicken Pizza for Meat Lovers

For those who crave the savory goodness of meat, the BBQ Chicken Pizza for Meat Lovers is a dream come true. This chapter explores how to combine different meats to achieve a symphony of flavors and introduces the mouthwatering BBQ Chicken and Sausage Pizza.

11.1 Combining Different Meats for Savory Bliss

The BBQ Chicken Pizza for Meat Lovers takes the indulgence of meat to the next level by combining multiple types of savory proteins. This medley of meats creates a rich and satisfying pizza experience that meat lovers will adore.

Ingredients:

- Prepared pizza dough (from Chapter 4)
- 1 cup cooked and shredded BBQ chicken
- 1/2 cup cooked and crumbled sausage (such as Italian sausage or chorizo)
- 1 cup BBQ sauce of your choice (from Chapter 3)
- 1 1/2 cups shredded mozzarella cheese
- 1/2 cup sliced red onions
- 1/4 cup sliced black olives
- Fresh parsley for garnish

Instructions:

1. Preheat your oven to the recommended temperature for pizza baking.
2. Roll out the pizza dough to your desired thickness and size.
3. Spread a layer of BBQ sauce over the pizza dough, leaving a small border around the edges.
4. Sprinkle half of the shredded mozzarella cheese evenly over the

sauce.

5. Spread the cooked and shredded BBQ chicken and crumbled sausage across the pizza.
6. Add the sliced red onions and black olives on top of the meats.
7. Finish with the remaining mozzarella cheese, ensuring all the toppings are well-distributed.
8. Transfer the pizza onto a preheated pizza stone or a baking sheet.
9. Bake the pizza in the preheated oven until the crust is golden and the cheese is bubbly and slightly browned.
10. Remove the pizza from the oven and let it cool slightly.

Before serving, garnish the pizza with fresh parsley, adding a burst of color and freshness to the savory blend of meats.

11.2 BBQ Chicken and Sausage Pizza

The BBQ Chicken and Sausage Pizza is the epitome of meat lover's delight, combining the succulent BBQ chicken with the hearty and flavorful sausage.

The tangy BBQ sauce beautifully complements the smokiness of the BBQ chicken and the robust flavors of the sausage. The combination of shredded mozzarella cheese, red onions, and black olives adds further depth to the pizza, creating a symphony of savory bliss with every bite.

Whether you're hosting a gathering with fellow meat enthusiasts or simply want to indulge in a pizza that celebrates the richness of meat, the BBQ Chicken and Sausage Pizza will satisfy your cravings for a hearty and satisfying meal.

Chapter 12: Making the Perfect Pizza Sauce

A delicious pizza sauce is the foundation of any great pizza, and in this chapter, we'll explore two fantastic options: a From Scratch Tomato Sauce and a Creamy Ranch Sauce specially crafted for BBQ Chicken Pizzas.

12.1 From Scratch Tomato Sauce

A From Scratch Tomato Sauce is a classic and versatile option that pairs perfectly with BBQ chicken pizza. This homemade sauce allows you to control the ingredients and tailor the flavors to your liking.

Ingredients:

- 2 tablespoons olive oil
- 1 small onion, finely chopped
- 2 garlic cloves, minced
- 1 can (28 ounces) crushed tomatoes
- 1 teaspoon dried oregano
- 1 teaspoon dried basil
- 1/2 teaspoon sugar
- Salt and pepper to taste

Instructions:

1. In a saucepan, heat the olive oil over medium heat.
2. Add the finely chopped onion and sauté until translucent, about 2-3 minutes.
3. Stir in the minced garlic and cook for an additional 30 seconds until fragrant.
4. Pour in the crushed tomatoes, dried oregano, dried basil, sugar, salt, and pepper. Stir to combine.
5. Reduce the heat to low and let the sauce simmer for 15-20

minutes, allowing the flavors to meld and the sauce to thicken.

6. Taste and adjust seasonings as needed, adding more salt, pepper, or herbs to your preference.

7. Remove the sauce from the heat and let it cool slightly before using it as a base for your BBQ chicken pizza.

The From Scratch Tomato Sauce brings a delightful balance of tanginess and sweetness to your BBQ chicken pizza. By making the sauce from scratch, you can ensure that it's free from unnecessary additives and preservatives, giving you a pure and authentic pizza experience.

12.2 Creamy Ranch Sauce for BBQ Chicken Pizzas

For a unique twist on traditional pizza sauce, a Creamy Ranch Sauce is a fantastic option for BBQ chicken pizzas. The creamy and tangy flavors of ranch dressing complement the smoky BBQ chicken, creating a delectable and satisfying combination.

Ingredients:

- 1/2 cup mayonnaise
- 1/4 cup buttermilk
- 2 tablespoons sour cream
- 1 teaspoon dried dill
- 1 teaspoon dried parsley
- 1/2 teaspoon garlic powder
- 1/2 teaspoon onion powder
- Salt and pepper to taste

Instructions:

1. In a mixing bowl, combine the mayonnaise, buttermilk, and sour cream, and whisk until smooth.
2. Stir in the dried dill, dried parsley, garlic powder, onion powder, salt, and pepper, blending everything together.
3. Taste the sauce and adjust the seasonings to your liking. You can add more dill, garlic powder, or other seasonings to suit your taste preference.
4. Once the sauce is well-balanced and flavorful, cover the bowl and refrigerate it for at least 30 minutes to allow the flavors to meld.

The Creamy Ranch Sauce is a delightful departure from the traditional tomato-based pizza sauce, offering a creamy and tangy alternative that pairs wonderfully with BBQ chicken and other toppings.

It adds a unique dimension of flavor to your BBQ chicken pizza, making it a standout creation that's sure to please your taste buds.

Chapter 13: Gluten-Free and Keto-Friendly Options

For those following a gluten-free or keto lifestyle, this chapter offers two delicious options: the Cauliflower Crust BBQ Chicken Pizza and the Low Carb BBQ Chicken Pizza. These recipes allow you to enjoy the flavors of BBQ chicken pizza while staying true to your dietary preferences.

13.1 Cauliflower Crust BBQ Chicken Pizza

Cauliflower crust has gained popularity as a gluten-free and lower-carb alternative to traditional pizza crusts. This Cauliflower Crust BBQ Chicken Pizza offers a nutritious and flavorful base that pairs perfectly with the tangy BBQ chicken.

Ingredients for Cauliflower Crust:

- 1 medium cauliflower head, grated or processed into fine rice-like texture
- 1 large egg, lightly beaten
- 1/2 cup shredded mozzarella cheese
- 1 teaspoon dried oregano
- Salt and pepper to taste

Instructions for Cauliflower Crust:

1. Preheat your oven to the recommended temperature for pizza baking.
2. Line a pizza stone or baking sheet with parchment paper.
3. Place the grated or processed cauliflower in a microwave-safe bowl and microwave for 5-6 minutes until it becomes tender.
4. Let the cauliflower cool slightly, then transfer it to a clean kitchen towel or cheesecloth. Squeeze out as much moisture as possible.

5. In a mixing bowl, combine the cauliflower with the beaten egg, shredded mozzarella cheese, dried oregano, salt, and pepper. Mix until well combined.
6. Transfer the cauliflower mixture onto the prepared parchment-lined pizza stone or baking sheet. Press and shape it into a thin, even crust.
7. Bake the cauliflower crust in the preheated oven for 15-20 minutes or until it becomes golden and slightly crispy around the edges.
8. Remove the crust from the oven and let it cool slightly before adding the BBQ chicken and toppings.

Once the cauliflower crust is ready, you can proceed with the toppings and BBQ chicken from your preferred recipe (such as the Classic BBQ Chicken Pizza from earlier chapters).

The Cauliflower Crust BBQ Chicken Pizza offers a nutritious and satisfying alternative to traditional pizza crust, allowing you to enjoy the flavors of BBQ chicken pizza without the gluten and excess carbs.

13.2 Low Carb BBQ Chicken Pizza

For those following a keto or low-carb diet, the Low Carb BBQ Chicken Pizza is a perfect choice. This version swaps the traditional pizza crust for a delicious low-carb alternative, keeping your carb intake in check.

Ingredients for Low Carb Pizza Crust:

- 1 cup shredded mozzarella cheese
- 1 cup almond flour
- 2 tablespoons cream cheese
- 1 large egg
- 1 teaspoon dried oregano
- Salt and pepper to taste

Instructions for Low Carb Pizza Crust:

1. Preheat your oven to the recommended temperature for pizza baking.
2. In a microwave-safe bowl, combine the shredded mozzarella cheese and cream cheese. Microwave on high for 1 minute, then stir well.
3. Return the cheese mixture to the microwave and heat for an additional 30 seconds until fully melted and combined.
4. In a separate mixing bowl, whisk together the almond flour, egg, dried oregano, salt, and pepper.
5. Add the melted cheese mixture to the dry ingredients and mix until a dough forms.
6. Place the dough between two sheets of parchment paper and roll it out into a thin, even crust.
7. Transfer the rolled-out crust onto a pizza stone or baking sheet lined with parchment paper.
8. Bake the low carb pizza crust in the preheated oven for 12-15 minutes or until it becomes golden and slightly crispy around

the edges.

9. Remove the crust from the oven and let it cool slightly before adding the BBQ chicken and toppings.

Once the low carb pizza crust is ready, you can proceed with the toppings and BBQ chicken from your preferred recipe (such as the Classic BBQ Chicken Pizza from earlier chapters).

The Low Carb BBQ Chicken Pizza caters to your keto or low-carb needs, offering a flavorful and guilt-free way to enjoy the beloved BBQ chicken pizza.

Chapter 14: Breakfast Twist: BBQ Chicken Pizza for Brunch

Who says you can't enjoy pizza for breakfast? In this chapter, we'll explore a mouthwatering Breakfast Twist to the classic BBQ Chicken Pizza, turning it into a delectable BBQ Chicken and Egg Breakfast Pizza. To add a touch of sweetness, we'll also introduce a Maple Syrup Drizzle that will elevate the flavors and make this brunch pizza an irresistible morning treat.

14.1 BBQ Chicken and Egg Breakfast Pizza

The BBQ Chicken and Egg Breakfast Pizza brings together the savory goodness of BBQ chicken with the richness of a perfectly cooked egg, creating a delightful morning indulgence.

Ingredients:

- Prepared pizza dough (from Chapter 4)
- 1 cup cooked and shredded BBQ chicken
- 1 cup BBQ sauce of your choice (from Chapter 3)
- 1 1/2 cups shredded mozzarella cheese
- 1/2 cup sliced red onions
- 2-3 large eggs
- Fresh cilantro or parsley for garnish
- Salt and pepper to taste

Instructions:

1. Preheat your oven to the recommended temperature for pizza baking.
2. Roll out the pizza dough to your desired thickness and size.
3. Spread a layer of BBQ sauce over the pizza dough, leaving a small border around the edges.

4. Sprinkle half of the shredded mozzarella cheese evenly over the sauce.
5. Spread the cooked and shredded BBQ chicken across the pizza.
6. Add the sliced red onions on top of the BBQ chicken.
7. Create small wells or indentations in the toppings to accommodate the eggs.
8. Carefully crack the eggs into the wells, ensuring the yolks remain intact.
9. Sprinkle a pinch of salt and pepper over the eggs.
10. Finish with the remaining mozzarella cheese, covering the toppings and eggs evenly.
11. Transfer the pizza onto a preheated pizza stone or a baking sheet.
12. Bake the pizza in the preheated oven until the crust is golden and the cheese is bubbly and slightly browned.
13. Remove the pizza from the oven and let it cool slightly.
14. Before serving, garnish the pizza with fresh cilantro or parsley, adding a burst of freshness to the breakfast delight.

The BBQ Chicken and Egg Breakfast Pizza is a perfect fusion of breakfast and dinner flavors, making it an ideal brunch treat that's sure to satisfy your morning cravings.

14.2 Maple Syrup Drizzle for Sweetness

To add a touch of sweetness to your BBQ Chicken and Egg Breakfast Pizza, a Maple Syrup Drizzle is the perfect finishing touch. This drizzle infuses the pizza with a delightful maple flavor, balancing the savory BBQ chicken and eggs with a hint of sweetness.

Ingredients:

- 1/4 cup maple syrup
- 1 tablespoon unsalted butter
- 1/2 teaspoon vanilla extract

Instructions:

1. In a small saucepan, melt the butter over low heat.
2. Stir in the maple syrup and vanilla extract.
3. Cook the mixture for 1-2 minutes, stirring continuously, until it slightly thickens.
4. Remove the saucepan from the heat and let the Maple Syrup Drizzle cool slightly.

To serve, drizzle the Maple Syrup over the cooked BBQ Chicken and Egg Breakfast Pizza just before serving. The sweetness of the maple syrup complements the BBQ chicken and eggs, creating a harmonious balance of flavors that will have you savoring each delightful bite.

Chapter 15: BBQ Dessert Pizza

Pizza doesn't have to be limited to savory flavors; it can be a delightful dessert as well! In this chapter, we'll explore two creative BBQ Dessert Pizza recipes that will satisfy your sweet cravings: the Decadent Nutella and BBQ Chicken Dessert Pizza and the Fruity Delight: BBQ Chicken and Berry Dessert Pizza.

15.1 Decadent Nutella and BBQ Chicken Dessert Pizza

Indulge in the perfect marriage of sweet and savory with the Decadent Nutella and BBQ Chicken Dessert Pizza. The combination of rich Nutella spread and tangy BBQ chicken creates an irresistible treat that's sure to become a favorite dessert.

Ingredients:

- Prepared pizza dough (from Chapter 4)
- 1/2 cup Nutella spread
- 1 cup cooked and shredded BBQ chicken
- 1/2 cup sliced bananas
- 1/4 cup chopped roasted hazelnuts
- Powdered sugar for dusting

Instructions:

1. Preheat your oven to the recommended temperature for pizza baking.
2. Roll out the pizza dough to your desired thickness and size.
3. Spread a generous layer of Nutella spread over the pizza dough, leaving a small border around the edges.
4. Sprinkle the cooked and shredded BBQ chicken evenly over the Nutella spread.

5. Add the sliced bananas on top of the BBQ chicken.
6. Sprinkle the chopped roasted hazelnuts over the pizza.
7. Transfer the pizza onto a preheated pizza stone or a baking sheet.
8. Bake the pizza in the preheated oven until the crust is golden and cooked through.
9. Remove the pizza from the oven and let it cool slightly.
10. Before serving, dust the pizza with powdered sugar for an extra touch of sweetness and visual appeal.

The Decadent Nutella and BBQ Chicken Dessert Pizza is a delightful combination of creamy Nutella, savory BBQ chicken, and crunchy hazelnuts, making it an exquisite dessert that will impress your family and friends.

15.2 Fruity Delight: BBQ Chicken and Berry Dessert Pizza

For a refreshing and fruity dessert pizza, the Fruity Delight: BBQ Chicken and Berry Dessert Pizza is a wonderful choice. The sweetness of the berries complements the tangy BBQ chicken, creating a balanced and vibrant flavor profile.

Ingredients:

- Prepared pizza dough (from Chapter 4)
- 1/2 cup cream cheese, softened
- 1 tablespoon honey
- 1 cup cooked and shredded BBQ chicken
- 1 cup mixed fresh berries (such as strawberries, blueberries, and raspberries)
- 1 tablespoon chopped fresh mint leaves

Instructions:

1. Preheat your oven to the recommended temperature for pizza baking.
2. Roll out the pizza dough to your desired thickness and size.
3. In a small bowl, mix the softened cream cheese and honey until well combined.
4. Spread the cream cheese mixture over the pizza dough, leaving a small border around the edges.
5. Sprinkle the cooked and shredded BBQ chicken evenly over the cream cheese layer.
6. Arrange the mixed fresh berries on top of the BBQ chicken.
7. Transfer the pizza onto a preheated pizza stone or a baking sheet.
8. Bake the pizza in the preheated oven until the crust is golden and cooked through.
9. Remove the pizza from the oven and let it cool slightly.
10. Before serving, sprinkle the chopped fresh mint leaves over the

pizza for a burst of freshness.

The Fruity Delight: BBQ Chicken and Berry Dessert Pizza offers a delightful combination of juicy berries, creamy cream cheese, and tangy BBQ chicken, making it a refreshing and satisfying dessert option.

Chapter 16: Aromatic Herbs and Seasonings

In this chapter, we'll explore how to elevate the flavors of BBQ Chicken Pizza with the addition of aromatic herbs and unique seasoning blends. These flavorful additions will take your pizza to a whole new level of taste and delight.

16.1 Elevating Flavors with Fresh Herbs

Fresh herbs are a fantastic way to add brightness and depth to your BBQ Chicken Pizza. They bring a burst of natural flavors that perfectly complement the tangy BBQ chicken and other toppings.

Some popular herbs that work wonderfully with BBQ Chicken Pizza include:

Fresh Basil: Basil's sweet and slightly peppery flavor enhances the overall pizza experience. Sprinkle torn or thinly sliced fresh basil leaves over your pizza after baking for a fresh and aromatic touch.

Fresh Cilantro: Cilantro adds a zesty and citrusy note that pairs well with the smokiness of BBQ chicken. Consider garnishing your pizza with chopped cilantro for a burst of freshness.

Fresh Parsley: Parsley has a mild and slightly bitter taste that can help balance the richness of BBQ chicken and cheese. Use chopped fresh parsley to add color and a subtle herbal flavor to your pizza.

Fresh Thyme: Thyme's earthy and slightly minty flavor complements the smoky BBQ chicken and savory toppings. Sprinkle fresh thyme leaves over your pizza before baking to infuse it with a delightful aroma.

Fresh Rosemary: Rosemary's bold and piney flavor adds a unique twist to BBQ Chicken Pizza. Use finely chopped fresh rosemary to elevate the taste of your pizza crust or as a garnish after baking.

Feel free to mix and match these fresh herbs or experiment with other aromatic herbs that you enjoy. Their addition will make your BBQ Chicken Pizza a truly herbaceous and delightful treat.

16.2 Unique Seasoning Blends for BBQ Chicken Pizza

To create a unique and unforgettable BBQ Chicken Pizza, consider incorporating custom seasoning blends that elevate the flavors and provide a personalized touch.

Here are a few seasoning blend ideas to try:

Smoky BBQ Seasoning: Create a blend using smoked paprika, garlic powder, onion powder, brown sugar, salt, and black pepper. This seasoning will intensify the smoky flavors of the BBQ chicken and add depth to your pizza.

Spicy Cajun Seasoning: Mix together cayenne pepper, paprika, garlic powder, onion powder, dried thyme, dried oregano, salt, and black pepper. This blend will infuse your pizza with a delicious Cajun kick.

Mediterranean Herb Seasoning: Combine dried oregano, dried basil, dried thyme, dried rosemary, garlic powder, salt, and black pepper. This Mediterranean-inspired blend will bring a herbaceous and aromatic flair to your pizza.

Tangy Lime and Chili Seasoning: Mix chili powder, lime zest, cumin, garlic powder, salt, and a pinch of cayenne pepper. This seasoning blend will add a tangy and slightly spicy twist to your BBQ Chicken Pizza.

To use these seasoning blends, simply sprinkle them over the BBQ chicken and other toppings before or after baking. The unique flavors will add an exciting dimension to your pizza that will impress your guests and leave them wanting more.

Chapter 17: Storing and Reheating Tips

To ensure that you can enjoy your BBQ Chicken Pizza to the fullest, this chapter provides valuable insights on how to store leftover pizza and creative ways to reheat it, preserving its delicious flavors and textures.

17.1 Keeping Leftover Pizza Fresh

Properly storing leftover pizza is essential to maintain its freshness and prevent it from becoming soggy or dry. Here are some tips to keep your BBQ Chicken Pizza tasting just as delicious the next day:

Refrigeration: If you have leftover pizza, refrigerate it promptly. Allow the pizza to cool to room temperature for about 30 minutes before transferring it to an airtight container or wrapping it tightly with plastic wrap. Refrigerate the pizza within two hours of its preparation.

Layering: To prevent the toppings from sticking together or becoming mushy, place a sheet of wax paper or parchment paper between each pizza slice before storing them in the container.

Airtight Containers: Use airtight containers to store your pizza. This helps retain its moisture and keeps it fresh for longer.

Best Use Within 3-4 Days: Consume your refrigerated leftover BBQ Chicken Pizza within 3-4 days for the best taste and quality.

Freezing: If you have a considerable amount of leftover pizza and you're unable to consume it within a few days, consider freezing it for longer storage. Wrap individual slices in plastic wrap and place them in a freezer-safe container or a resealable freezer bag. Properly frozen pizza can be stored for up to 2-3 months.

17.2 Creative Ways to Reheat BBQ Chicken Pizza

When it comes to reheating BBQ Chicken Pizza, microwaving it often results in a soggy crust and unevenly heated toppings. Instead, try these creative methods to reheat your pizza while maintaining its deliciousness:

Oven or Toaster Oven: Preheat your oven or toaster oven to around 375°F (190°C). Place the pizza slices directly on the oven rack or on a baking sheet lined with parchment paper. Reheat for 8-10 minutes or until the cheese is bubbly, and the crust becomes crispy again.

Skillet or Pan: Heat a non-stick skillet or frying pan over medium-low heat. Place the pizza slices in the skillet and cover it with a lid. Reheat for 3-4 minutes or until the cheese melts and the crust crisps up.

Grill or BBQ: For a unique and smoky touch, reheat your BBQ Chicken Pizza on a grill or BBQ. Preheat the grill to medium heat and place the pizza slices directly on the grates. Reheat for 3-4 minutes or until the toppings are hot and the crust is nicely charred.

Air Fryer: If you have an air fryer, it can be an excellent way to reheat pizza with minimal effort. Place the pizza slices in the air fryer basket and heat them at 350°F (175°C) for 3-4 minutes or until warmed through and crispy.

Panini Press: If you own a panini press, it can be used as a convenient and effective tool to reheat pizza. Simply place the pizza slices on the preheated panini press and cook for 2-3 minutes until the cheese is melted and the crust is toasted.

By using these creative reheating methods, you can enjoy your BBQ Chicken Pizza as if it were freshly made, with a crispy crust and flavorsome toppings.

Chapter 18: Hosting a BBQ Chicken Pizza Party

Hosting a BBQ Chicken Pizza Party is a fun and interactive way to bring people together to enjoy delicious food and great company. In this chapter, we'll guide you through creating a DIY Pizza Station and offer beverage pairing suggestions to make your BBQ Chicken Pizza Party a memorable and enjoyable event for all.

18.1 Building a DIY Pizza Station

A DIY Pizza Station allows your guests to get creative and personalize their own BBQ Chicken Pizzas. It adds an element of fun and ensures that everyone gets to enjoy their favorite toppings. Here's how to set up a fantastic DIY Pizza Station:

Pizza Dough: Provide a variety of pizza dough options, such as traditional, whole wheat, gluten-free, and low-carb crusts. You can either make the dough yourself (using the recipes from earlier chapters) or purchase pre-made dough from a store.

BBQ Chicken and Toppings: Prepare plenty of BBQ chicken and a variety of toppings to suit different tastes. Offer options like shredded mozzarella cheese, sliced red onions, black olives, bell peppers, fresh basil, pineapple chunks, jalapeño slices, cooked bacon, and more.

Sauce Options: Set up different sauce options to cater to various preferences. Offer classic tomato sauce, Creamy Ranch Sauce (from Chapter 12), and even a bowl of BBQ sauce for those who want an extra tangy kick.

Pizza Assembly: Provide rolling pins, flour, and clean surfaces for guests to roll out and shape their pizza dough. You can also provide pizza peels or baking sheets to help transfer the pizzas to the oven.

Baking Area: If possible, set up an outdoor pizza oven or grill for a fun and authentic pizza-making experience. Alternatively, a preheated indoor oven works well too.

Toppings Bar: Arrange the toppings and sauces in separate containers with serving spoons. Label each container to make it easy for guests to identify their choices.

Personalization: Encourage your guests to get creative and experiment with different combinations of toppings. Offer serving platters for guests to showcase their unique BBQ Chicken Pizzas.

With a DIY Pizza Station, your BBQ Chicken Pizza Party will become an interactive and enjoyable culinary experience for everyone.

18.2 Pairing Beverages with BBQ Chicken Pizza

Pairing the right beverages with your BBQ Chicken Pizza is crucial to enhance the flavors and create a well-rounded dining experience. Here are some beverage suggestions to complement the savory and tangy flavors of BBQ Chicken Pizza:

Craft Beer: Opt for craft beers with a touch of bitterness and hoppy notes. IPAs (India Pale Ales) or Pale Ales work well with BBQ Chicken Pizza, as they cut through the richness and complement the smoky flavors.

Red Wine: Choose a medium-bodied red wine with fruity notes, such as a Zinfandel or a Merlot. The fruitiness and mild tannins of these wines complement the tanginess of the BBQ sauce and the richness of the cheese.

Lemonade or Iced Tea: For a non-alcoholic option, refreshing beverages like lemonade or iced tea pair wonderfully with the smoky and tangy flavors of BBQ Chicken Pizza.

Sparkling Water with Citrus: Provide sparkling water infused with lemon, lime, or orange slices for a refreshing and palate-cleansing option that complements the pizza's flavors.

Homemade Lemonade: Offer a homemade lemonade station with different flavored syrups, such as raspberry or lavender, for guests to customize their own lemonade concoctions.

Remember to offer a variety of beverage options to cater to different preferences and dietary restrictions. Encourage your guests to explore the different pairings and find their perfect match with BBQ Chicken Pizza.

Chapter 19: Beyond Chicken: BBQ-Style Veggie Pizzas

While BBQ Chicken Pizza is a classic favorite, exploring BBQ-style veggie pizzas can be a delightful and flavorful twist. In this chapter, we'll introduce two mouthwatering options: BBQ Cauliflower Pizza and BBQ Portobello Mushroom Pizza. These veggie-centric creations will satisfy both vegetarians and meat-eaters alike.

19.1 BBQ Cauliflower Pizza

BBQ Cauliflower Pizza offers a delicious and nutritious alternative to traditional meat toppings. The roasted cauliflower takes on a smoky flavor from the BBQ sauce, creating a delectable and satisfying pizza.

Ingredients:

- Prepared pizza dough (from Chapter 4)
- 2 cups cauliflower florets, chopped into bite-sized pieces
- 2 tablespoons olive oil
- Salt and pepper to taste
- 1/2 cup BBQ sauce of your choice (from Chapter 3)
- 1 1/2 cups shredded mozzarella cheese
- 1/4 cup sliced red onions
- 1/4 cup fresh cilantro, chopped

Instructions:

1. Preheat your oven to the recommended temperature for pizza baking.
2. In a mixing bowl, toss the cauliflower florets with olive oil, salt, and pepper until well coated.
3. Spread the cauliflower on a baking sheet lined with parchment paper.
4. Roast the cauliflower in the preheated oven for 20-25 minutes

or until it becomes tender and slightly charred.

5. Roll out the pizza dough to your desired thickness and size.

6. Spread a layer of BBQ sauce over the pizza dough, leaving a small border around the edges.

7. Sprinkle half of the shredded mozzarella cheese evenly over the sauce.

8. Add the roasted cauliflower and sliced red onions on top of the cheese.

9. Finish with the remaining mozzarella cheese, covering the toppings evenly.

10. Transfer the pizza onto a preheated pizza stone or a baking sheet.

11. Bake the pizza in the preheated oven until the crust is golden and the cheese is bubbly and slightly browned.

12. Remove the pizza from the oven and let it cool slightly.

13. Before serving, garnish the pizza with fresh cilantro for a burst of freshness.

The BBQ Cauliflower Pizza is a flavorful and wholesome option that's sure to impress your guests and make even the most devout meat-lovers fall in love with veggie-based pizza.

19.2 BBQ Portobello Mushroom Pizza

For a hearty and meaty texture, BBQ Portobello Mushroom Pizza is an excellent choice. The marinated and grilled portobello mushrooms add a savory element that perfectly complements the tangy BBQ sauce.

Ingredients:

- Prepared pizza dough (from Chapter 4)
- 4 large portobello mushroom caps, cleaned and stems removed
- 2 tablespoons olive oil
- 2 tablespoons balsamic vinegar
- 2 garlic cloves, minced
- Salt and pepper to taste
- 1/2 cup BBQ sauce of your choice (from Chapter 3)
- 1 1/2 cups shredded mozzarella cheese
- 1/4 cup sliced red bell pepper
- 1/4 cup sliced red onions
- 1/4 cup crumbled feta cheese
- Fresh parsley or basil for garnish

Instructions:

1. Preheat your grill to medium-high heat.
2. In a small bowl, whisk together olive oil, balsamic vinegar, minced garlic, salt, and pepper to create a marinade.
3. Brush the portobello mushroom caps with the marinade on both sides.
4. Grill the portobello mushrooms for 4-5 minutes on each side until they are tender and slightly charred. Once grilled, slice the mushrooms into thin strips.
5. Roll out the pizza dough to your desired thickness and size.
6. Spread a layer of BBQ sauce over the pizza dough, leaving a small border around the edges.
7. Sprinkle half of the shredded mozzarella cheese evenly over the

sauce.

8. Add the grilled portobello mushroom strips, sliced red bell pepper, and sliced red onions on top of the cheese.
9. Finish with the remaining mozzarella cheese and crumbled feta, covering the toppings evenly.
10. Transfer the pizza onto a preheated pizza stone or a baking sheet.
11. Bake the pizza in the preheated oven until the crust is golden and the cheese is bubbly and slightly browned.
12. Remove the pizza from the oven and let it cool slightly.
13. Before serving, garnish the pizza with fresh parsley or basil for a pop of color and flavor.

The BBQ Portobello Mushroom Pizza is a hearty and satisfying option that brings a rich and savory twist to BBQ-style veggie pizzas, making it a delightful addition to your pizza party.

Chapter 20: Final Thoughts and Culinary Adventures

Congratulations on completing "The World of BBQ Chicken Pizza" cookbook journey! As we conclude this culinary adventure, let's delve into some final thoughts on customizing your own BBQ Chicken Pizzas and exploring global BBQ pizza inspirations.

20.1 Tips for Customizing Your Own BBQ Chicken Pizzas

Creating your own BBQ Chicken Pizzas is a delightful way to experiment with flavors and tailor the pizzas to suit your personal preferences. Here are some tips for customizing your pizza creations:

Toppings Galore: Get creative with toppings! Mix and match different ingredients like caramelized onions, roasted garlic, fresh spinach, artichoke hearts, or even sliced apples for a unique and flavorful pizza experience.

Cheese Varieties: While mozzarella is a classic choice, feel free to use other cheese varieties like cheddar, gouda, goat cheese, or feta to add distinct flavors to your pizzas.

Spice It Up: If you enjoy heat, consider adding sliced jalapeños, red pepper flakes, or hot sauce to your BBQ Chicken Pizza for an extra kick.

Sweet and Savory Combos: Explore sweet and savory combinations by incorporating ingredients like fresh fruits (pineapple, peaches, or figs) or drizzling honey over your pizza to complement the tangy BBQ sauce.

Herbaceous Flair: Enhance the pizza's aroma and taste by using a variety of fresh herbs like basil, cilantro, rosemary, or thyme.

Play with Crusts: Experiment with different pizza crusts, such as cauliflower crust, gluten-free options, or even using naan bread or tortillas as a base for quick and easy personal-sized pizzas.

Remember, there are no limits to customizing your BBQ Chicken Pizzas, so let your culinary creativity soar and craft pizzas that excite your taste buds!

20.2 Exploring Global BBQ Pizza Inspirations

As you become well-versed in the art of BBQ Chicken Pizza, why not embark on culinary adventures that draw inspiration from global flavors? Take your BBQ pizzas to new heights by exploring different regional influences:

Korean BBQ Pizza: Incorporate Korean barbecue flavors by marinating the chicken in a bulgogi-inspired sauce, adding kimchi, and drizzling a gochujang-infused BBQ sauce over the pizza.

Indian Tandoori Pizza: Embrace the Indian flavors of tandoori chicken by marinating the chicken in yogurt and a blend of tandoori spices, and then topping the pizza with red onions, bell peppers, and a drizzle of mint chutney.

Mediterranean BBQ Pizza: Infuse your pizza with Mediterranean charm by using marinated grilled chicken, kalamata olives, sun-dried tomatoes, artichoke hearts, and a sprinkling of feta cheese.

Mexican BBQ Pizza: Embrace Mexican flavors by using BBQ-seasoned chicken, black beans, corn, avocado, and a drizzle of chipotle aioli.

Thai-inspired BBQ Pizza: Create a Thai-inspired pizza with lemongrass-marinated chicken, coconut milk-infused BBQ sauce, and toppings like red bell peppers, Thai basil, and crushed peanuts.

Venturing into global BBQ pizza inspirations adds excitement to your culinary repertoire and allows you to experience the delicious diversity of international flavors.